Calico Cats

by Meredith Dash

www.abdopublishing.com

Published by Abdo Kids, a division of ABDO, P.O. Box 398166, Minneapolis, Minnesota 55439.

Copyright © 2015 by Abdo Consulting Group, Inc. International copyrights reserved in all countries. No part of this book may be reproduced in any form without written permission from the publisher.

Printed in the United States of America, North Mankato, Minnesota.

052014

092014

 THIS BOOK CONTAINS RECYCLED MATERIALS

Photo Credits: Pixabay, Shutterstock, Thinkstock

Production Contributors: Teddy Borth, Jennie Forsberg, Grace Hansen

Design Contributors: Candice Keimig, Laura Rask, Dorothy Toth

Library of Congress Control Number: 2013952415

Cataloging-in-Publication Data

Dash, Meredith.

Calico cats / Meredith Dash.

p. cm. -- (Cats)

ISBN 978-1-62970-008-3 (lib. bdg.)

Includes bibliographical references and index.

1. Calico cats--Juvenile literature.   I. Title.

636.8--dc23

2013952415

Table of Contents

Calico Cats

Calico cats are not a **breed**.

They are a color pattern.

4

5

Calicos are three colors. They are white, black, and orange.

7

The three colors appear in patches. White is the most noticeable color.

9

Any **breed** of cat can be a calico cat. Persian cats can be calico.

Scottish folds can be calico.

Maine coons can be calico too.

13

Male calico cats are **rare**. Calicos are almost always female.

Personality

Every calico cat is different.

Its **personality** depends on

its **breed**.

Grooming

Like all cats, calicos should be brushed weekly. This will keep their coats healthy.

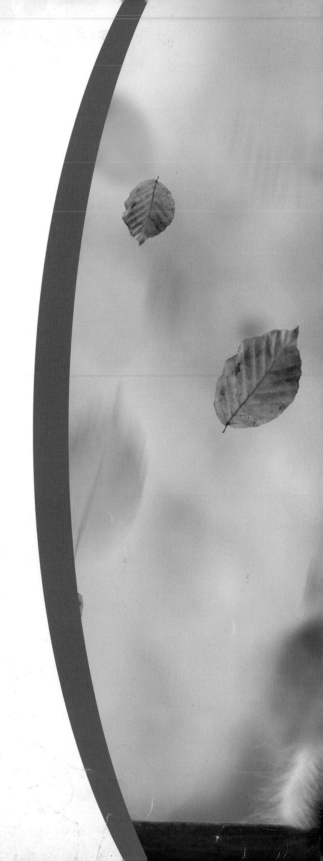

Lucky Cats

Old tales say that calicos bring good luck. Most people feel lucky to own this beautiful cat.

20

21

More Facts

- Calicut, India was known for its cotton-weaving center. Calico cloth is named after Calicut. The cloth had **patches** of different colors. This is how the calico cat got its name.

- Male calico cats are **rare** and unhealthy.

- The calico cat is the state cat of Maryland. Calicos have the same coloring as Maryland's state bird (the Baltimore oriole) and insect (the Baltimore checkerspot).

Glossary

breed – a group of animals sharing the same looks and features.

noticeable – easily spotted.

patch – a small piece of fur that is a different color.

personality – how one acts.

rare – not usual.

Index

abdokids.com

Use this code to log on to abdokids.com and access crafts, games, videos and more!

Abdo Kids Code:
CCK0083

24